W9-CZK-090

CLASSIC WISDOM COLLECTION

TODAY'S QUESTIONS. TIMELESS ANSWERS.

Looking for time-tested guidance for the dilemmas of the spiritual life? Find it in the company of the wise spiritual masters of our Catholic tradition.

Christ in Our Midst: Wisdom from Caryll Houselander

Comfort in Hardship: Wisdom from Thérèse of Lisieux

Courage in Chaos: Wisdom from Francis de Sales

Inner Peace: Wisdom from Jean-Pierre de Caussade

Intimacy in Prayer: Wisdom from Bernard of Clairvaux

Life's Purpose: Wisdom from John Henry Newman

Path of Holiness: Wisdom from Catherine of Siena

Peace in Prayer: Wisdom from Teresa of Avila

Secrets of the Spirit: Wisdom from Luis Martinez

A Simple Life: Wisdom from Jane Frances de Chantal

Solace in Suffering: Wisdom from Thomas à Kempis

Strength in Darkness: Wisdom from John of the Cross

Christ in our Midst

Christ in Our Midst

Wisdom from Caryll Houselander

Compiled and with a foreword by Mary Lea Hill, FSP

Pauline
BOOKS & MEDIA
Boston

Library of Congress Cataloging-in-Publication Data

Houselander, Caryll.
  Christ in our midst : wisdom from Caryll Houselander / compiled and with a foreword by
Mary Lea Hill, FSP.
      pages cm
  Includes bibliographical references.
  ISBN-13: 978-0-8198-1632-0
  ISBN-10: 0-8198-1632-9
  1. Jesus Christ--Face. I. Hill, Mary Lea, editor of compilation. II. Title.
  BT590.P45H68 2013
  242--dc23

                                    2013016790

Scripture quotations are transcribed from the original translations of Caryll Houselander's works.

Excerpts from Caryll Houselander's works are published by Bloomsbury Publishing, United Kingdom. Reprinted with permission.

> *A Rocking-Horse Catholic*, copyright © 1955 by Sheed & Ward
>
> *The Mother of Christ*, copyright © 1978 by Sheed & Ward.
>
> *The Comforting of Christ: Being a Peace-Time Edition, rev. and enl. ed. of*
> *This War Is the Passion*, copyright © 1947 by Sheed & Ward.
>
> *The Flowering Tree*, copyright © 1945 by Sheed & Ward.
>
> *Guilt*, copyright © 1951 by Sheed & Ward
>
> *The Passion of the Infant Christ*, copyright © 1949 by Sheed & Ward.
>
> *This War Is the Passion*, copyright © 1941 by Sheed & Ward.
>
> *The Risen Christ*, copyright © 1958 by Sheed & Ward.
>
> *The Dry Wood*, copyright © 1947 by Sheed & Ward.
>
> *The Reed of God*, copyright © 1944 by Sheed & Ward.
>
> *The Letters of Caryll Houselander: Her Spiritual Legacy*, edited by Maisie Ward,
> copyright © 1965 by Sheed & Ward.

Cover design by Rosana Usselmann

Cover photo by Mary Emmanuel Alves, FSP

"P" and PAULINE are registered trademarks of the Daughters of St. Paul.

Published by Pauline Books & Media, 50 Saint Pauls Avenue, Boston, MA 02130-3491

Printed in the U.S.A.

www.pauline.org

Pauline Books & Media is the publishing house of the Daughters of St. Paul, an international congregation of women religious serving the Church with the communications media.

1 2 3 4 5 6 7 8 9   17 16 15 14 13

To my uncle Mark Delano Hill

Contents

Foreword

I'm staring at the pattern on the rug and I distinctly see the forehead, hairline, cheeks, chin, eyes, brows, and the hint of a mouth. It's not someone I recognize, just a face. Fortunately it isn't Jesus, Mary, or Mother Teresa, so I won't cut out the section to sell online, nor will I turn the living room into a shrine. It is just a face, or the facsimile of a face, as illusive as the shapes seen in clouds on a lazy summer's day. One look away and the image vanishes.

So, why a face? Why not hands, feet, or even the back of a head? I suspect it is because people are fascinated by faces, which can reveal or conceal so much.

Faces connect us and also identify us. One evening I was having dinner with my cousins, all of them daughters of the same aunt and uncle. The question came up: "Which of us do you think looks most like our mother?" The two of them who strongly resemble their father were not in contention, but the other four were in the running. I immediately blurted out one name only to see other faces fall. Later that evening, it occurred to me that one of the others was almost a spitting image of her mother. And really, all four of them carried a striking resemblance to her, varied but true.

It is these variations that make families so interesting. How many combinations and interpretations result from the faces of one man and one woman? It's genetic magic. In a sense, Caryll Houselander worked a similar marvel in the many and compelling ways she presented the face of Christ, the one face we all long for. As a weaver of words and a deeply mystic soul, Caryll saw the face of Christ everywhere: as he is in the Church, as he hides in the needy or speaks through the poor, as he suffers in the sinner, as he serves, searches, and stands up in the midst of everyday life, as he lives in each one of us. Every book, every article she wrote aimed at making us aware of this wonderful truth: a definite family resemblance is found among believers.

My first encounter with the writings of Caryll Houselander was a hurried, last-minute scan of *The Reed of God*, which had been assigned summer reading. I didn't get much out of it. I didn't pay attention to any of her writings until years later. In a visit to my Uncle Mark, a self-professed "Houselander groupie," I discovered something I had overlooked so long ago. My uncle summarized the message of his kindred spirit. He sent me home with several of her books, which I then read eagerly. I found that in everything she wrote her intention was to show us how much we all look like Christ and are part of the great mystery known as his Mystical Body. Her life's work was to help us understand the implications of this mystery.

Frances Caryll Houselander was, by her own admission, a very detached child. This was due in great part to her tumultuous childhood. She was born on September 29, 1901, in Bath, England, the second daughter of Gertrude Provis and Wilmott Houselander.[1] Caryll was six years old when Gertrude suddenly awoke to religion and was baptized Catholic together with her daughters. Unfortunately, long prayers and external devotions were overemphasized while the family's foundation disintegrated. Nothing of the trouble was discussed with the children. Caryll's imagination and nervous sensitivity propelled her to find refuge in a world of her own making, full of poetic images and tall tales.

With the breakup of the family, the Houselander girls were thrust into the unfamiliar life of boarding school, where Caryll withdrew further. She was frequently ill and her formal schooling suffered. With time, however, she warmed to her surroundings and developed an attachment to the French nuns who ran the school.

During these early years Caryll had her first mystical experience. She happened upon a religious sister, a Bavarian, truly a misfit in wartime England, who was weeping. Out of respect Caryll turned away, but turning back she was stunned, and exclaimed, "*I* would not cry, if I was wearing the crown of thorns like you are."[2]

Years later on a trip to the market, Caryll experienced the whole sky illumined by a dazzling icon of the face of Christ the King crucified. And her final great vision took place on the London subway, where she was suddenly confronted by Christ visible in each passenger. She was quick to say these were not things she actually saw, but things present to her soul. Prior to this last vision, Caryll, an art student, had entered into the idealistic world of protests and freethinking. She had been offended by the pettiness and lack of charity among believers and opted out of the formal practice of her faith. She had been in and out of love and even had an affair with a famous English spy.[3] However, as she began to note the presence of Christ in each person, she was drawn back to the Church. Then, instead of rebelling against the evils and injustices she witnessed on the streets of London, Caryll involved herself in relieving them, one person at a time. She created the Loaves & Fishes, a society whose members engaged in secret acts of charity toward the poor. Writing, illustrating, and woodcarving barely provided for her support. However, her life grew more settled when she became acquainted with a young divorcee, Iris Wyndham, who invited Caryll to live with her, thus saving Caryll from likely destitution.

During the Second World War, Caryll joined several home defense activities, including watching for enemy bombers at night. When her writing became successful, she responded by giving more freely. Her fame also brought to her door numbers of people in search of advice. Some London psychologists entrusted difficult patients to her for counseling because they recognized her ability to love them back to life, a gift she attributed to the fact that she was neurotic herself. Although painfully shy in crowds, she was the delight of her close friends, always laughing and joyful, and an entertaining storyteller, actress, and mimic.

With all this, was Caryll perfect? Not if you consider her chain smoking, affection for a stiff drink, or penchant for the quick, cutting remark. She *was* perfect, however, in her effort to show Christ to the seeker through her own way of living the Gospel and the "Host-life," that is, the gift of self for others.

After this short, but remarkably gifted and giving life, Caryll died of breast cancer on October 12, 1954.

Who was Caryll Houselander, really? I would like to say she was a prophet of our eternal connectedness. She wrote endlessly, haranguing and hurrahing us with the realization that Christ wishes to live in us, to be one body with us.

Caryll exemplifies how daring Our Lord is in his dealings with a person when he wants cooperation. And just as Christ laid claim to Saint Paul's learning and zeal, with Caryll it was her insight and her style. Both Paul and Caryll were allowed to see Jesus, and both were then asked to give him to their contemporaries. Caryll generously dove into this mission, spending her physical and creative energies in showing us the beauty and nearness of Christ, his presence in the Church, in the world, in self, and in each person we encounter, whether saint or sinner. She used the reality of everyday life to illustrate the mystery of the life to come. She helped us examine the life of grace, which flows through our collective lives and binds us together.

We all know people who have separated themselves from the Body of Christ. They consider the Church irrelevant, and this is always painful to witness. As believers we want to hold the family of faith together. Therefore, when someone asks where they can find Christ today, what do we say? Where do we point? Added to the ordinary trials of life, the Church may look unappealing, even appalling, so where are people to find God? Where will they see Christ? Caryll says the answer must begin with us, within us. "The only certain way of giving truth to others is by *showing* Christ to them in ourselves. People now are too tired and disintegrated to think, too unconcentrated to read serious books, too disillusioned to be moved by abstract theories, too unstable to listen to logical arguments, too much hurt to endure exhortation—*they must see!*"[4]

By her own admission Caryll Houselander was an oddity, an eccentric person who used all her natural and supernatural gifts to draw others toward their true destiny. She could be seen in the streets of London, her smiling face covered with a strange white paste, her eyes peering through her round glasses, her striking red hair bouncing with each step. She gave of herself totally and joyfully to all whom she encountered. Her life abounded in acts of kindness toward both friend and stranger. She never shied even from acting the fool to bring joy to a troubled soul. She would counsel us to be conduits of all the love and the pain, the doubt and the faith of our contemporaries. From her we can learn to put ourselves out there, quirks and all, as the loving, inviting face of Christ today.

I

The Choice

Suppose that God gave every man the choice between a world in which there was no suffering, but also no capacity for love, or a world in which suffering remains, but everyone has the power to love. Which do you think mankind would choose? Which would *you* choose? Quite certainly the power to love, even at the cost of suffering.

Now this is precisely what has happened. The thing which makes us able to love is free-will, and it is the same thing, free-will, which makes us able to sin. Without it there would be no sin and no love in the world.

— *The Mother of Christ*, 80

II

The Responsibility

The responsibility of all the love of all the ages of the world belongs to each one, through each one flows the whole torrent of life that is given from generation to generation by love: love, which through the miracle of the Incarnation is made tangible and audible in us, so that its music is heard in our voices—in the plighting of our troths, in our marriage vows, in our words of comfort and pity and joy, in our laughter, in the songs beside our cradles, in our choirs of adoration; love, which we transmit with our touch, with the work of our hands, with the labors and pains, the ecstasies and the embraces of our bodies, in the act of procreation, of giving birth, in nursing and serving, and in closing the eyes and bathing the limbs of our dead; love, which holds the timelessness of God in a moment of time, which—with the sacramentals of our flesh and blood, our hands, our voices, our hearts, our minds—forgives, redeems, heals, generates, adores.

To attempt to repress Christ in ourselves is to attempt to hold back the river of life, to stop the bloodstream of the Son of God that is the lifestream of all mankind.

The man in whom Christ is not repressed is a channel through which the life and love of all humanity flows back to God. And as the bloodstream in a man's body is purified by the air he breathes, his supernatural life is purified by the breath of the Spirit that perpetually renews the life of Christ in man. It flows through the divine Mind and through the heart of mankind, continually purifying human nature of the poison that has infected it, perpetually renewing the life of the world.

— *Guilt, 96–97*

III

God in Us

What is Love? Many people think and some of them say so, that it is sexual passion. That certainly is a superb expression of love. But it is not the whole of love, and it is quite possible to have sexual passion without any love at all. In this regard, many people—with blasphemy that is pitiful because it is unconscious and because, too, they are speaking of the best they know—say "God is love," meaning "God is license."

There is a wistful belief that love has a power to make people something, to reform them, to make them noble. That is true of real love. But the purely natural love, with its alloy of self, does not make one anything, it merely shows exactly what one is. Love is sometimes responsible for heroism, but it is sometimes responsible for crime too.

It is true that God is love—but it is a truth which can be more easily grasped if we say Love is God.

When God enters into our passions, joys, desires, sorrows, into our relationship with one another, our nature undergoes a transubstantiation. The Paraclete Who rests in the human heart changes the substance of our humanness to Christ, we are charged with the power of Christ's love. Love is God in us.

This power of love is the beginning of the world's healing, of human happiness. The world is made up of weak as well as strong people, of dull as well as intelligent people, of blind people as well as those who have vision, of naturally superficial as well as intense people. If all these and the millions more are to be as one, are to find happiness that is good and is a hallowing of God's Name, they must do it in the only way they can: through the interchange in daily life of the love of Christ.

In love the world has life. This is yet another reason why we need the revelation, the truth told by Christ. Love must be governed by law.

How chill that sentence must fall on many burning hearts who think law is a series of prohibitions; that the way to Heaven is like the way to Berlin in a pre-war German train, "Verboten" written large wherever we look![1] Something restricting and crushing love. On the contrary, God's law is a natural law, which simply concentrates the meaning and force of love and gives the love of every individual a lasting and abiding beauty. It is to life what the law of verse is to poetry. Without the rules of rhythm and sound and harmony, the pause, the stress, the silences, the words of a poem have no meaning. Let them fall apart and be mixed up and spoken at random, and what you have is something more like the raving of a lunatic than the expression of a lover. But gather them into the order and strength and discipline of poetry, and you have an expression of love which not only tells the splendor of one poet's heart, but one in which all the inarticulate of the world speak for ever.

Such concentration and power of love, safeguarded and made enduring by a musical law, can restore humanity to happiness.

If we accept Christ's words, the communion of love between all the people and ultimately all the peoples in the world is the interchange of Christ's love; it is, therefore, the continual giving and taking and increase of creative life. It is Christ giving Himself through us, the ultimate expression between us of the humility from which we started, which, knowing self as part of a whole and the whole as Christ, realizes the potency, the peace, that is in both the vastness and the littleness of all that we do and are.

There is no problem which love cannot solve, no wound which it cannot heal, no wrong which it cannot forgive, no passion which it cannot sanctify. There is no place where it cannot be practiced, no circumstances from which it cannot radiate, no living of it which does not answer the world's need and which is not a giving of life to all men.

The kiss of the bride and the bridegroom is Christ's kiss of peace to the world; the mother nursing her baby is a symbol of God holding the world to His heart. Love is Christ giving Himself through us, in our hands, in our words, in our tenderness, in our restraint, in all that we do, in all our communions with one another.

A young man setting his pace to an old man's footsteps is love; a swift thinker curbing his thoughts for a slow mind is love. The ascetic fasting that the world may be fed is love; the celibate offered to God that marriages be holy is love; the patience that cherishes the sick and the lonely is love; the sickness suffered sweetly for the world is love. The boy who is decent to the new boy at school is love; the toleration that makes home pleasant to the young is love; the charity that judges no sinner is love; the fortitude that compromises with no sin is love. It is the Christ giving between us all.

— *The Comforting of Christ*, 9–12

IV

Paradox of Love

In the fact of loving at all, there is for us, fallen creatures, an element of suffering. We realize the frailty of those we love, the million evil chances that threaten them. We are haunted by the fear of loss, of parting. By a strange paradox, falling in love brings us a new realization of our own nothingness, our helplessness to do, even to be, what we would for the beloved. Only the sacrament of matrimony in which in a mysterious way God re-creates two as one, in his own love, can overcome this nothingness. But we live in a world that is de-Christianized, divorced from love's very self; so marriage, for most people, involves material hardship and self-denial if they would live in obedience to God.

The lover is like the craftsman: he has to give himself to years of discipline, of patient work and perseverance, in order to attain his skill. There must be countless new beginnings, the exacting process of habit-forming, with its repeated denials of self, until at last his mind and eye and hand work in harmony on the material that he knows, as he knows his own soul. Just so is the lot of the lover, who has life for his material, life that sin has twisted, so that it is like wood that is knotted and warped. Yet on this material he acquires the skill that makes the craftsman an artist and enables him to fashion his own life into a thing of sheer beauty, and not his own life only, but the lives of those dear to him. Inevitably, in the process, he will have enlarged and strengthened his heart and mind; his hand will have become sensitive and capable, his eyes will be the trained eyes that see the loveliness of the world, that others are blind to. His home will be the little house that is built upon a rock, which stands fast when the rains come and the winds blow and the houses built upon sand are swept away.

. . . The dying to self which makes our love like Christ's is not selfless; selfless love would not be love at all; but it is the surrender of self in our love. It is the reverse of selfish love, which is, after all, only self-love. Many who imagine that they love are really concerned with nothing else but being loved.

— *The Risen Christ*, 15–17

V

Being Godlike

There is a widespread idea today that it does not matter what our conception of God is like; how vague it is, how confused, even how distorted. "We all worship the same God" has become almost a shrug of the shoulders, dismissing the responsibility of knowing God as He reveals Himself to be, as if to know Him truly made no difference to us.

But as our conception of God is, so we ourselves become. If we think He is hard, we grow hard; if we think He is a kill-joy we become kill-joys, if we think of Him as an omnipotent secret police, all-present, all-seeing, all-terrible, we shrink from Him, and the heart that shrinks from God shrinks to nothing.

Saddest of all misconceptions is the merely negative God; it is this that fills the world with negative, apathetic people, futile before the misery of mankind. Only Christ's light can touch that misery. Only in that light shining within us can we see the long-obscured path back to human happiness and walk in it.

. . . What the world needs is to see. Even a blind man can see a bright light through his darkness. We can give the light of God to the world by giving our hearts to the light of God.

Christ's way is unchanging, He comes into the world through individual lives. In the individual heart is the world's redemption. He comes to those who desire Him, to the heart that is given to Him to shelter His light, and to each He comes as He came to Mary, for the whole world. He is not confined by our limitations or hidden by our darkness, His light irradiates from our heart and illuminates the world, He is always the light that shines in darkness.

— *The Mother of Christ*, 48–50

VI

Scandal

To young and inexperienced people a single word or gesture can produce an emotional reaction which has unimaginable consequences; certainly, before one is twenty these often thoughtless incidents are more effective than any reasoning. Such a one precipitated a crisis for me. One morning, quite by chance, I knelt at Holy Communion side by side with two people, a husband and wife, who had in the past been acquainted with my mother and the priest she now harbored.[1] They were highly respected Catholics. After Mass I greeted them in the church porch. They ignored my greeting and turned away.

From that moment I made up my mind to seek for some other religion. I did not doubt the Real Presence in the Blessed Sacrament, but it seemed to me that Christ was a prisoner in the hands of hard and relentless people, people without compassion. I began to hope that there might be some other church in which there would also be the Real Presence, but in which one could approach and receive Christ, not among respectable people, not among censorious people, but among those who were despised, who were failures, who were sinners, but who loved one another. That "good Catholics" should receive Communion side by side with one whom they immediately cut dead, appalled me. It appalled me that it was into the hands of such that, so it seemed to me, Christ had given Himself— "this night you will all be scandalized in Me."[2]

— *A Rocking-Horse Catholic*, 104–5

VII

Who Am I?

Every person living is—besides being one of the human race—*himself*; and in order to make the raw material of *himself* what it *is*, innumerable different experiences and different influences have been used.

. . . We are often reminded that we have been chosen by God out of innumerable potential people whom He did not create. But very seldom do we think about the mystery of all the years and all the people and all the gathered memories, both of individuals and races, which have made us individually what we are.

Our life has been given to us from generation to generation, existing in each age in the keeping of other human beings, tended in the Creator's hands . . . .

. . . It is a great mistake to suppose that those who have inherited the material for their life from suffering generations, and who have poor health and a timid approach or some vice or weakness, have not been designed and planned by God as much as others who seem luckier in the world's eyes.

. . . Each one of us—as we are at the moment when we first ask ourselves: "For what purpose do I exist?"—is the material which Christ Himself, through all the generations that have gone to our making, has fashioned for His purpose.

— *The Reed of God*, 5–7

VIII

The Young Man

There is a young man
who lives in a world of progress.
He used to worship a God
Who was kind to him.
The God had a long, white beard.
He lived in the clouds.
But, all the same,
He was close to the solemn child
who had secretly
shut Him up in a picture book.
But now
the man is enlightened.

Now he has been to school
and has learnt to kick a ball
and to be abject
in the face of public opinion.
He knows, too,
that men are hardly removed from monkeys.
You see, he lives in the light
of the twentieth century.
He works twelve hours a day
and is able to rent a room
in a lodging house
that is not a home.
At night he hangs
a wretched coat
upon a peg on the door
and stares
at the awful jug and basin
and goes to bed.
And the poor coat,
worn to the man's shape—
round-shouldered and abject—
watches him, asleep,
dreaming of all
the essential,
holy things
that he cannot hope to obtain

for two pounds ten a week.
Very soon
he will put off his body,
like the poor, dejected coat
that he hates.
And his body will be
worn to the shape
of twelve hours' work a day
for two pounds ten a week.
If he had only known
that the God in the picture book
is not an old man in the clouds,
but the seed of life in his soul;
the man would have lived,
and his life would have flowered
with the flower of limitless joy.
But he does not know,
and in him
the Holy Ghost
is a poor little bird
in a cage,
who never sings
and never opens his wings,
yet never, never
desires to be gone away.

— *The Flowering Tree*, 14–16

IX

Making Life Holy

Emptiness is a very common complaint in our days, not the purposeful emptiness of the virginal heart and mind but a void, meaningless, unhappy condition.

. . . The purpose for which human beings are made is told to us briefly in the catechism. It is to know, love, and serve God in this world and to be happy with Him for ever in the next.

This knowing, loving, and serving is far more intimate than that rather cold little sentence reveals to us.

. . . It is impossible to say too often or too strongly that human nature, body and soul together, is the material for God's will in us.

There are many people in the world who cultivate a curious state which they call "the spiritual life." They often complain that they have very little time to devote to the "spiritual life." The only time that they do not regard as wasted is the time they can devote to pious exercises: praying, reading, meditations, and visiting the church.

All the time spent in earning a living, cleaning the home, caring for the children, making and mending clothes, cooking, and all the other manifold duties and responsibilities, is regarded as wasted.

Yet it is really through ordinary human life and the things of every hour of every day that union with God comes about.

— *The Reed of God*, 1, 4–5

X

Visions

I have already told you about the Bavarian lay sister in my French convent whom I saw crowned with thorns.

What do I mean by saying that "I saw"? Frankly, in the ordinary way I did not *see* anything at all; at least I did not see anything with my eyes . . . . I saw her *with my mind* wearing the crown of thorns, and saw this vividly in detail, in a way that is unforgettable, though in fact it was something suddenly *known*, rather than seen.

. . . It was such an experience that I had on that night in July 1918, one which I now know to have been linked with the first . . . .

I was on my way to buy potatoes . . . . Suddenly I was held still, as if a magnet held my feet to a particular spot in the middle of the road. In front of me, above me, literally wiping out not only the grey street and sky but the whole world, was something which I can only call a gigantic and living Russian icon. I had never seen a Russian icon at the time, nor, I think, any reproduction of one. I have seen very many since, but none that has approached this one in beauty.

It was an icon of Christ the King crucified.

. . . In spite of the early teaching of the French convent that humiliation can be the way to the glory of God, I had failed to accept the humiliations that had been heaped upon me; my heart had contracted, my mind narrowed. As most humiliated and self-centered people do, I resented not only those people who had in fact snubbed me, but those who possessed what I lacked; and like most of those who are vain and secretly scourged by awareness of their own inferiority, my inclination was rather to drag people down to my level, if I could, than to make any effort to lift myself up to theirs.

. . . I had set my face against the rich, whom I supposed to be "the idle" classes, and was becoming more and more anti-clerical, with a growing dislike for every hierarchy.

Now suddenly, between one heartbeat and the next, I had seen the drama and reality of Christ's Passion in kings.

. . . It was not for nothing that my first glimpse of Christ in man was in the humblest of lay sisters, bowed by a great crown of thorns, and my second a king in splendor, bowed under a great crown of gold. I realized that every crown is Christ's crown, and the crown of gold is a crown of thorns.

— *A Rocking-Horse Catholic*, 111–12, 114–16

XI

Other Christs

Christ said, "Without me you can do nothing,"[1] and we see how true this is. How could we imitate an example of uncompromising unworldliness, chastity, sacrifice, and love, offered two thousand years ago by someone we have never seen, when we are unable to keep our promises to people we know well and saw yesterday, and instinctively belittle the qualities of our more heroic friends because we dislike and resent the fact that their example challenges our rationalization of the line of least resistance?

Of course we could but fail if we were merely trying to *imitate* Him.

But that is not what is asked of us, and that is not the meaning of Christianity. What we *are* asked to do is to be made one with Christ, to allow Him to abide in us, to make His home in us, and gradually, through the oneness that results from living one life, and through the miracles of His love, consummated again and again in Communion with Him, to *become* Christs, to live in Him as Our Lady did. When we are changed into Him as the bread into the Host, then with His power we can follow His example.

This seems to make the question of our inconsistency stranger than ever, because all those inconsistencies are the result of having a misconception of what Christ is like, and it seems almost impossible not to know what someone is like if you share a room with him.

We all know that there is a tendency to skip or skim through those passages in the Gospel which disconcert us, and to form a conception, not only of Christ, but of His special relationship to ourselves, by the passages which are as we say most "consoling" to us.

When I hear Christians discussing economics, I remember a figure who often loomed in my childhood; a very large figure, too, seated squarely and heavily in an armchair on one of the several famous green lawns in her grounds. At her side is a box of sodamint,[2] and a little way behind her back, her acquaintances, whispering—between yawns and within hearing of the child among them taking notes—that her prodigious wealth was derived from the rents of slums. Now this old lady was exacting in piety and a devoted reader of the Bible; whether she ever read any other passages, I do not know, but the passage that she always read to me was the one in which "The Lord is my Shepherd: I shall not want" occurs.[3]

We all tend to that sort of scripture reading. And though we do not depend only on reading, yet it is really necessary, in our search for Christ, to read the Gospel, and to read it all without flinching; or if we must flinch, at least without giving up the attempt.

— *The Reed of God*, 79–80

XII

Mystical Relationships

I remember one day asking an old man outside Saint Paul's Cathedral, where I spent my hungry lunch hour, to give me a piece of the bread with which he was feeding the pigeons. He refused, because, he said, he loved birds, not people! This answer puzzled me. My own attitude to people had radically changed since I had seen the "Russian icon," and since the necessity of earning my living had forced me to go out and meet all kinds of people. I was still tormented by morbid shyness and a distressing consciousness of being "peculiar" myself, but in spite of that, people—those I knew and those I did not know—fascinated me in an extraordinary, even an obsessive way. I felt that somehow, in some way not yet clear to me, there must be a kind of mystical relationship between people, a bond which was wholly independent of exterior things; a kind of relationship which enabled all to help all, even though they were not acquainted. This, like so much else in my life, came to me through odd flashes and intuitions. It was not a thought-out thing at all.

. . . Every night at about ten o'clock, when I was sitting huddled on my bed in the dark, I heard the tap, tap, tap of a blind man's stick, passing below in the street. It had an extraordinary effect on me. Somehow, between me and this unknown blind man there was an affinity. Was I not spiritually blind? Was I not, too, tapping, here, there and everywhere, longing for light, but feeling my way in darkness, because the darkness was not in the night that was lit by the splendor of the stars, but in my own soul? I began to pray for this blind man—and I had almost lost the habit of prayer.

I began, too, to feel an urge to go out and walk about at night among the London crowds. Until now my interest had been in two sorts of people—those whom I actually knew personally, and the far-off Russians, of whom I was always conscious, as people living through the Passion in our own days. Now—curious as it may seem—because of this blind man, who I had never seen, tapping with his stick in the night, I wanted to go out and rub shoulders with the London crowds. In some sort of way, which I could not yet define, I wanted to *take part* in these countless lives that I began to realize as pressing on me.

— *A Rocking-Horse Catholic*, 128–30

XIII

Christ Everywhere

I was in an underground train, a crowded train in which all sorts of people jostled together, sitting and strap-hanging—workers of every description going home at the end of the day. Quite suddenly I saw with my mind, but as vividly as a wonderful picture, Christ in them all. But I saw more than that: not only was Christ in every one of them, living in them, dying in them, rejoicing in them, sorrowing in them—but because He was in them, and because they were here, the whole world was here too, here in this underground train; not only the world as it was at that moment, not only all the people in all the countries of the world, but all those people who had lived in the past, and all those yet to come.

I came out into the street and walked for a long time in the crowds. It was the same here, on every side, in every passer-by, everywhere—Christ.

. . . The "vision" lasted with that intensity for several days, and each of them revealed the mystery and its implications for me a little more clearly. Although it did not prevent me from ever sinning again, it showed me what sin is, especially those sins done in the name of "love," so often held to be "harmless"—for to sin with one whom you loved was to blaspheme Christ in that person; it was to spit on Him, perhaps to crucify Him. I saw too the reverence that everyone must have for a sinner; instead of condoning his sin, which is in reality his utmost sorrow, one must comfort Christ who is suffering in him. And this reverence must be paid even to those sinners whose souls seem to be dead, because it is Christ, who is the life of the soul, who is dead in them; they are His tombs, and Christ in the tomb is potentially the risen Christ. For the same reason, no one of us who has fallen into mortal sin himself must ever lose hope.

It would be impossible to set down here all the implications of this "vision" of Christ in man; it altered the course of my life completely, and in a sense took away my difficulty about the Blessed Sacrament's being put into the hands of sinners. I saw that it is the will of Christ's love *to* be put into the hands of sinners to trust Himself to men, that He may be *their* gift to one another, that *they* may comfort Him in each other, give Him to each other. In this sense the ordinary life itself becomes sacramental, and every action of anyone at all has an eternal meaning.

— *A Rocking-Horse Catholic*, 137–39

XIV

The Tomb

The modern world is the tomb of Christ. Sometimes we feel inclined to echo the question of the mourners in Jerusalem: "Who is to roll the stone away for us?"[1] so heavy are the circumstances which seem to prevent the resurrection we long for.

Faith is our most urgent need today. Not vague aspirations, but clear-cut, definite faith in what Christ said. Faith that we can follow like a map. For many the meaning of the word is forgotten. Some imagine that they have faith because though they doubt the virgin birth, they enjoy Christmas carols; some because they hope confusedly for a Christian state with higher wages and no restriction on individual sin.

To work, to hope, to live for less than complete Christianity, to accept a compromise, to lose confidence in man's capacity for goodness, is to deny our faith.

Christ has faith in man. He said that he was salt, giving savor to life that would be flat and tasteless without Him. He said that He was the light of the world,[2] burning out across the darkness. He said that He would make His own home in man's soul and even make him one with God the Father.[3] If that is Christ's faith in man, we must at least believe in the potential Christ in every man alive.

. . . If we judge by the newspapers, it would seem that Christianity is a failure. Famine, cruelty, suspicion, threats, fear, violence, crime. This after two thousand years of Christianity! Certainly it looks like a failure. What did it look like when Christ was in the tomb? Christ had claimed to be the life of the world—He was dead. He had promised His people a kingdom, He had been hanged outside the city. He had claimed to be king, He had been crowned with thorns. Only a handful of men had kept their faith in Him and the handful had fled. One of them had even denied that he knew Him, another had sold Him for a contemptible fee. He was stripped naked, made mock of, He died with nothing of His own, even His grave was borrowed. Certainly it looked as if Christ was a failure.

At that time the faith of the whole world was kept alive by a few devoted women. Even the apostles doubted them when they told them (what they should have known) that Christ had kept His word. "But to their minds the story seemed madness and they could not believe it."[4]

Those women believed it because they had the faith which discovers through love. They had never wanted any earthly triumph for Christ, never expected it. They believed in Christ the poor man, the forsaken man, even the crucified man. If they could not have Christ with all His humiliations and stripes, they would not seek to comfort themselves with anything else. So they came, asking who would roll back the stone, to find it already removed and Christ alive, with the wounds our sin had inflicted on him blazing like stars in his risen body.

Today it is in the Catholic Church that faith in the resurrection is kept alive. Often enough too, some pious old woman is the keeper of the church's faith, faith that is nourished by intimate personal love for the suffering Christ—the very tender love that seeks for Christ, crucified in man.

— *The Mother of Christ*, 69–71

XV

The Reception

Hunger for life burnt visibly on their lifted faces, and Timothy had an answer to that hunger in his soul, for on the very day that the green leaf broke into life on the stunted tree, he had been received into the Catholic Church.

. . . The charwoman who swept and dusted the church witnessed his reception.

. . . "Don't worry now," she said. "You'll feel better when you've made your confession; and mind you, tell the whoppers first, and when it's all over you shall have a nice cup of tea, as you won't be going to your Holy Communion until tomorrow. Oh, I've seen many young men, and a few old ones, come into the Church. Same as I've seen lots of people come into the world, and go out of it . . . . "

Timothy nodded. He knew with emotionless joy that the candle of Faith that the priest put into his hand was the candle that would be burning by his coffin, that the hands he folded now, he folded over his dead heart, that the will that he pledged was the gift both of his life and the homage of the dust.

He said his Act of Faith like a child reciting a lesson, and when it was all over, and he made the Sign of the Cross on leaving the church, he realized the wonder of the sign, and marveled, but still impersonally, as if he was thinking of another man. He was going back to the office now, in the name and the power of the Trinity!

He, the hollow man, who an hour ago had no power at all. He looked and felt just the same as before, but before he was powerless, now he was going out in the power of Christ's love!

He saw the significance, the shape and the size of the Sign of the Cross as he would not see it again, covering him, his mind, his shoulders, his heart. He saw it now objectively, as we only see what is new to us, as we see new faces, new people, whom, when we know and love or hate, we shall see changed by our own conception of them, or shall not see at all, because they have been taken too close.

Now he saw the shape of the cross, man's mind the shaft of it pointing heavenward, and he saw his shoulders taking on the world's suffering in Christ's power and his arms reaching out to left and right in the stretch of his mercy, and his heart—the center of the great road, and the source of his love, the horizontal beam driving down into the earth, and the sap of life rising up from its roots.

He walked to the office, and no red flowers sprang up out of the pavement where he walked, and there was nothing at all to mark the wonder of the day.

But on that day the leaf pierced the hard wood of the little black tree with life, the tree that was rooted in the poor, sooty earth of the London square, and there was a voiceless *"Sursum Corda,"* "up with your hearts," in the city.[1]

— *The Dry Wood*, 117, 119–20

XVI

Delight in the Lord

No one can fail to see when a friend has fallen in love and to guess, from the effects, with what sort of person they *are* in love. If that person is good, kind, reliable, then the lover will come alive, they will sing at their work, they will have confidence, they will glow with a new warmth, a new tenderness. Everything round them will remind them of the person they love, so nothing will be dull or meaningless, their very face will change. The plainest face is beautiful when it is lit from within by love.

Their friends will think them lucky to be loved by this person whom they have not met, but whose character is so clearly shown by the new life, the radiant beauty of the one who is loved; if their own life happens to be bleak, drab, loveless, they will think wistfully how different *they* would be if they too were loved like this!

The implication is obvious; the littleness of the individual stressing the glory of God is His revelation to the world. No one need be wistful for His love. "Here," they can say, "is someone as weak and ordinary as I am, living my life, but their communion with Christ has made them joyful and vital and beautiful, it is an invitation to me to take Him to my heart too and live in His life."

That is the eucharistic life—giving our littleness to God and rejoicing in Him, through our littleness giving Him to the world.

"Delight in the Lord and He will give you the desires of your heart."[1]

— *The Mother of Christ,* 36–37

XVII

Christ-life in the Soul

The basic idea of Catholicism *is* the indwelling of the Holy Spirit in man, the Christ-life in the soul, and all that this implies, both as regards a man's conduct in his own life and his charity to other men. I am sure that you would be absorbed if you got one or two books on the subject written by good theologians and studied them. I am *not* a theologian and not very well fitted to expound on doctrine, but as I understand it, the doctrine is this: that in every baptized Christian (which means anyone baptized at all, not only those baptized by a Catholic priest, and includes those who have the baptism of desire and of blood)[1]—in the soul of every baptized Christian, Christ lives. He is, as it were, a germ of Christ in them, or a seed of Christ. This seed of Christ grows and flowers in them as they correspond to grace, and the whole object of a Christian is to become "another Christ"—that means, to become Christ: the word "other" or "another" is used just to remind us that though we are capable of being absolutely one with Him, there *is* all the same an otherness about God, otherwise we couldn't adore and serve Him; also though, through grace, we are identified with Him, this is a free gift won for us by the Incarnation of Christ, and we are still men dependent on Him for our very being.

— Letter to Elizabeth Billaux, September 30, 1935,
The Letters of Caryll Houselander: Her Spiritual Legacy, 8–9

XVIII

Christ's Mystical Body

Deep in the heart of everyone living is the longing to be in communion with other men. It is this longing which gives even selfish people an instinctive wish that they were of the fiber that is willing to bear its share of the common burden of effort and hardship.

. . . In Christ, all those who are members of his Mystical Body are one in a way that our generation, divided and torn as it is, can hardly imagine. It is a far closer oneness than that of husband and wife, of a mother and her unborn child—of a man with his own thought.

We are one as the different parts of a human body are one because in them all there is one life. The bloodstream that flows through the human body gives life to the brain and the heart, to every limb and organ, to the tips of the fingers—not a multiplication of lives, but one.

The cause of this oneness is that all the members of Christ's Mystical Body *live with his life.*

. . . Perhaps it is because of the tremendous implications—and sometimes terrible implications—of this mystery that many pious people prefer to shrink into themselves and their own devotions rather than to allow the whole wonder of their life in Christ to break down every barrier to the uncompromising charity which it commits them to.

It means that nothing whatever that one member of the Church does is without its effect on all the others.

— *Guilt*, 94–95

XIX

I Am My Brother

It is time that Christians put aside the self-protective type of religion, with its interminable formalities and pious exercises and its careful exclusions and respectable cliques, and recognized *Christ and themselves* in the disreputable members of the Church; the socially ostracized, the repulsive, the criminals, the insane; the drifting population of the streets and the doss-houses,[1] the drug addicts and drunkards; the man waiting in the condemned cell to die—and the tiresome, thankless, and dissolute members of a man's own household. It is time that Christians answered Cain's question "Am I my brother's keeper?"[2] by more than an affirmative: "I am more than that, *I am my brother.*"

To *each* man who lives in Christ, *all* men belong, all love and wisdom and joy, all suffering and fear and atonement, all power and beauty, all living and dying, all childhood and manhood. Because Christ is whole in each member of His Body on earth now, each in a sense is the Mystical Body. He is in a sense all humanity. Each man owes his tears for his own sins to every other man, and each owes the joy of Christ to every other. The Christian in whom Christ lives has in himself all men, the child in him is capable of understanding all the dreams and fears and mystery of all childhood, the lover in him the love of all manhood.

The responsibility of *all* sin is upon the shoulders of each Christian man.

We cannot escape from Christ, the destiny of our being. We can open our minds, abandon our will to the mystery—or refuse to do so, and live in conflict with Christ, and therefore in conflict with our own life, struggling, as the majority are doing today, to repress Christ in our souls, to dam up our life, and to doom the human race with the doom of a city divided against itself.

To accept, to abandon ourselves to our destiny as "other Christs," is not only to allow all the grief and suffering of the world to flow through us, but also eternal love, love that has no beginning in time and does not end in time: love that has no limitation of place, or act, that does not depend upon the accidents of our lives, though it can be expressed through them too.

— *Guilt*, 95–96

XX

The Risen Christ

The ultimate miracle of Divine Love is this, that the life of the Risen Lord is given to us to give to one another. It is given through our own human loves. It is no violation of our simple human nature. It is not something which must be cultivated through a lofty spirituality that only few could attain; it does not demand a way of life that is abnormal, or even unusual; it is not a specialized vocation. It is to be lived at home, at work, in any place, any circumstances. It is to be lived through our natural human relationships, through the people we know, the neighbors we see. It is given to us, if we will take it, literally into our own hands to give. It is the love of human lovers, of man and wife, of parent and child, of friend and friend.

It is through his Risen Life in us that Christ sends His love to the ends of the earth. That is why instead of startling the world into trembling adoration by manifesting His glory, He sent the woman who had been a sinner to carry the ineffable secret,[1] and sent the two disciples who had been bewildered by their blind inability to reconcile Scripture and Calvary,[2] and sent the friend who had denied Him,[3] to give His love to the world, and to give it as simply as a whispered secret or a loaf of bread. So is it that we, sinners, wranglers, weaklings, provided only that we love God, are sent to give the life of the Risen Christ to the whole world, through the daily bread of our human love.

— *The Risen Christ*, 11–12

XXI

Secret Glory

At first sight the most astonishing thing about the risen life is its ordinariness. But that is wholly consistent with Christ's way. His revelation of Himself was always gradual, always told like a secret. Before knowing Him as God, He wanted men to know Him as themselves, so that they would not be afraid to come close to Him. Now He is determined that His incredible experience of having died and come back shall not make a barrier. There must be no sense of the uncanny to awe His apostles.

He will not even startle them by letting them realize suddenly, unwarned, that He is there. They must first realize that they are with someone ordinary, and afterward learn who it is. His greeting is always a reassurance. He is concerned by so human a thing as whether they have something savory to make their dry bread palatable. He lights a fire and cooks a little breakfast for them Himself. His way of making His identity known shows how well He knew "what was in the heart of man." He knew what each individual needed to make their share in the joy of His resurrection possible.

Peter is not asked to say that he is sorry, only to reassure himself and Christ that he really does love Him in spite of those denials. It is a fact that makes the mind dumb with wonder that Christ always wanted to be reassured of people's love. It mattered more to Him than anything they had done to wrong Him, in fact nothing else mattered at all. Magdalene knew Him by the mingled tenderness and restraint with which He greeted her; both things were her dire need. Thomas, the forerunner of all those who do not agree that seeing is believing, must touch the wounds in His body. The disciples going to Emmaus were first given light on the whole subject of Christ's suffering, light that glowed within them. Afterward they knew Him in the breaking of bread.

. . . Our Lord gave Himself to us through our flesh and blood, we give ourselves back to Him through it. The symbols of the gift of His own life are bread, wine, water, and oil. We give our life back to Him through the dust He made us out of, through everything we see and touch and taste and hear, the food we eat, the clothes we wear, the words we speak, the sleep we sleep. Such are the sacramentals of our love, things ordinary with the ordinariness of the risen Christ.

Our apostolic life, and not to be apostolic is not to be Christian, is just as ordinary. Our communion with one another, which is our Christ-giving to one another, is in eating, working, sharing the common sorrows and responsibilities, comforting one another in soul and body, talking to one another.

The Catholic Church has a secret to reveal. The Church is not only the hierarchy but all the people, sinners as much as saints, foolish and wise, the young, the mature, the old, little children, rich and poor, strong and weak. All of us. The secret is, Christ risen lives in us. Certainly He has continued His policy of not letting His identity be obvious! We must copy His way if anyone is ever to recognize Him.

. . . Today . . . the glory is still secret, but it is a secret that is communicated to millions, through the simplest substances of life and the hourly practice of love. Resurrection is in the hearts of those who love, the heart of Christ beginning to beat in them.

— *The Mother of Christ*, 72–74

XXII

Reaching Sanctity

Father O'Grady reflected sadly that Father Malone would gradually fade from their memory. As the old people died one by one, bit by bit the memory of the saint would die with them.

. . . And what, Father O'Grady asked, smelling the foul old pipe tenderly, could make such things the substance of sanctity? These things that belong so inevitably to the limitations of human nature? Surely Christ's presence in men. Surely because God breathed on the dust and took flesh and blood from a human creature, and worked and ate and slept and loved on earth.

Because the Word is made flesh and we behold His glory, in the least and the lowliest.

Yes, Father O'Grady knew it now; that was the secret of Father Malone's sanctity, Christ's presence. He was a saint to his people, because he was a Christ to his people; in the end he had worn his humanity, worn himself, like an old coat, so threadbare that his bones showed through it almost visibly, but it was not his bones that showed at all, it was the shape of Christ, Who had hallowed the name of God in his old bones.

Father Malone's sanctity had simply been Christ's, "Here am I who have been all this while in your company: hast thou not learnt to recognize me yet?"[1]

And Riverside had had its moment of transfiguration; the door into heaven had stood open; Riverside had reflected the light of glory. For a moment the people had laid hold of the feet of snow that shone upon Tabor,[2] and then the glory had faded. Now there was no one there but "Jesus only"—the hard work, the poverty, the sorrow and love, the Word made flesh.

Father O'Grady looked at his watch. The server was late. He checked a feeling of irritability, and was shocked by the difficulty he felt in checking it.

Was sanctity within *his* reach after all, he asked; could his great hands lay hold of it after all, he who never knew the sweetness of the complete act of love, the unbroken prayer, the whole hour of meditation, the work accomplished, the sensible sweetness of the sacramental word spoken, even one hour out of the twenty-four, unbroken, for his personal delight!

Could he who never knew that completeness in his soul, that inward closed circle of light, be a saint?

Could his day of fragments be a day in a saint's life?

And the answer came to him, paralyzing in its beauty: this broken life of his was the breaking of the bread, that in the broken bread, the Whole Christ be given to his people. Soon, in a few minutes now, his people would be at the altar rails, opening their mouths like sparrows for their Crumb of Life, and in their Crumb of Life they would receive all Life, whole.

. . . And the priest was on the side of life, he had no other work, no other raison d'être but to give life, and the life he gave could not be killed. He was not outside of the world's love because he was a priest and alone, he was the heart of the world's love, its core, because the Life of the World is born every day in his hands at Mass.

— *The Dry Wood*, 246–49

XXIII

The Approach of Christ

Christ never forced His love on anyone. Though He is perfection, he never allowed himself to dominate the will and mind of another with his own. He desired love that would be a communion, closer than human marriage, closer than the life of a mother to her unborn child, an unimaginable communion of love, but all were to come to it through their own experience, in their own way; even, by a positive miracle of mercy, through their own imperfections, through the experience of their weakness and need, through sorrow for their sins.

The impulse was to begin for each one in his own heart. It was never to be a violation of the individual soul;

instead, a gentle, almost imperceptible, movement of inward life. It could be likened to the quickening of the seed in the earth, when the warmth and light of the sun which is burning in heaven comes down through the darkness and enters into it, and the tender green shoot pushes towards the light, compelled by the very sun that is so far away, and yet is within it.

In the five recorded incidents of Christ appearing in His Risen Body, He allowed each of those to whom He showed Himself to discover that it was He in their own way, through their own medium. His approach to them, always exquisite in courtesy, miraculous in humility, was in each case one that showed His intimate knowledge of each one individually. He knew which would be the most natural way for that particular person to respond to His love, and what each needed to lift his or her heart from the sorrow or shame which was crushing it and restore it to the joy that would enable it to enter into communion with Him.

— *The Risen Christ*, 38–39

XXIV

Be the Gospel

If a chance occurs, we shall explain our faith; at all events we shall be able to. We shall have to know it so well that it is in our blood, and to adhere to it so well that we can in a certain way give it, just by being what we are. Thus we must be the book of the Gospels ourselves, with the words and teachings of Christ in our minds, but also in our hearts, and whenever the occasion demands, upon our lips. That is something that the daily Mass reminds us of constantly, when we make the triple Sign of the Cross before the Gospel.

We shall have also to be the flowering of Christ, the continuing of His love, and in this way we are like the bread for the Host, sacramental. It may be hard to go to confession, it may be difficult to hear Mass, to receive Communion . . . . Then will be the time when we, who have long used the sacrament of penance, taking God's forgiveness over and over again, will ourselves give continual life in the world to this expression of Christ, forgiveness. We will do it by forgiving, by forgiving whatever needs forgiveness, day after day.

— *This War Is the Passion*, 10

XXV

The Flowering of Christ

If Christ is growing in you, you are growing toward sacrifice. If the spirit of sacrifice is not growing in you, Christ is not growing in you, no matter how ardently you may think of Him or how eloquently you may speak of Him. But if day after day your life gathers to a culmination of sacrifice, then it is certain that Christ waxes strong in you.

A sacrifice is not, as so many people imagine, a mortification; it is not something that is meritorious according to its degree of unpleasantness; on the contrary, in real sacrifice, there is joy which surpasses all other joys, it is the crescendo and culmination of love.

What is a sacrifice?

A girl of eleven, asked to teach a child of four to "make a sacrifice," taught him to make the Sign of the Cross. Asked why this should be a sacrifice, she answered with supreme wisdom, "Because for a little minute he gives all of himself to God."

. . . The child shuts his eyes with an effort, he screws up his whole face to keep them shut; this is perhaps the hardest part of it, to give up for a few moments the bright and lovely toys that are enchanting him. Christ closed His eyes upon the lilies of the field and the wild birds and all the world that was bright and lovely and dear to Him as to no other man.

When we make a sacrifice it is always thus, we have to give something up, not because it is a bad thing—for more often it is a good thing—but the offering of ourselves is a complete offering, it means a whole attention, a whole concentration, a whole donation.

. . . Christ was more than a connoisseur of all the loveliness of the world; on all of it He closed His eyes to die.

The hands that He stretched out to the nails were strong, capable, craftsman's hands; the body He offered was the body of a young man in the perfection of young maturity; the mind that was then crowned with thorns was the mind of a philosopher and poet, an intellect that could never be equaled.

It seemed, I suppose, a waste. The world so needed men like Christ. Even had He not been God, He would have been among the few who can do so much. He could make men see life in a new way; He gave vision as well as sight; He could make the common life, the workman's life, so splendid, he was such a psychologist, He understood what was in the heart of man—and then He could work miracles!

But for all that, He chose to die, He sacrificed Himself. Closing His eyes, He closed them not only on the flowers that were drenched with His blood at the foot of the cross but on the faces of His mother and friends, who looked up at Him; in giving Himself to God, He gave up everything.

— *The Comforting of Christ*, 12–15

XXVI

Showing Christ

The knowledge that we are part of Christ's body, His living body, which is all Christians, should make humility of the mind inevitable and the practice of humility its logical result.

It should make us equally glad to have the highest place or the lowest, to do the most splendid or the humblest task, not because we are indifferent and don't mind what we do, but because whatever we do is something that Christ is doing.

For Christ cannot act in conflict with Himself. There is in Him the flow and sweetness of order and harmony, perfect as pure music, and it is clear that, using Saint Paul's imagery,[1] His mind and heart are doing what His hand is doing. In the tiny threadlike capillary in His little finger flows the blood that sweeps through His heart.

. . . We may be the fingertips of the Mystical Body of Christ, working among the little and lowly because they most need His healing, and through us He can best heal. . . .

Humility itself, if it is really knowing oneself to be part of the Mystical Body of Christ, depends on revealed Truth. No one could have guessed or discovered the Mystical Body; we only realize it because Christ told it to us;[2] it is the core of revealed Truth. In its light we see the meaning of our own lives, the proportion and value of our every act, and we can, if we look outside of ourselves, see in the light of the same mystery the meaning of other lives and deaths, of the martyrs of our own century, the suffering of children and so on.

Possibly we may start by accepting only with the heart, the fact of Christ in us, and our life in Christ, our minds may not have yet taken full hold of it; but the experience of living this fact leads to a tremendous will to accept anything at all that Christ has revealed, knowing it must be for the peace and the fullest possible life of the world, of all humanity. Any actual personal experience of any part of the Truth of God, leads on to this readiness of the heart to receive the whole Truth.

If we already have been given the grace of Truth, if, though we cannot imagine why, *we* have been brought up in the Catholic faith, we ought to pray daily, even hourly in our days, to be allowed in spite of ourselves to be part of the answer to those who *are* crying out, "Lord, that I may see!"

For the only certain way of giving truth to others is by *showing* Christ to them in ourselves. People now are too tired and disintegrated to think, too unconcentrated to read serious books, too disillusioned to be moved by abstract theories, too unstable to listen to logical arguments, too much hurt to endure exhortation—*they must see!*

— *The Comforting of Christ*, 2–5

XXVII

Seeing Christ

We must learn to see Christ in others with the eyes of faith, because the whole orientation of our will, in which is the secret of peace, will depend upon whether we *act* as if we did see Christ in them or not.

It is part of God's plan for us that Christ shall come to us in everyone; it is in their particular role that we must learn to know Him; He may come as a little child, making enormous demands, giving enormous consolation; He may come as a stranger, so that we must give the hospitality to a stranger that we should like to give to Christ; He may come to us in His Passion, disfigured by our sins and all sin, asking the utmost courage of us, that we may not be scandalized and may believe. He may come to us as a servant and compel us to the extreme of humility which accepts His service, as Peter had to do, when He washed his feet, and as the disciples did with unquestioning joy, when He cooked their little meal on the seashore.

If we see everyone in our life as "another Christ" we shall treat everyone with the reverence and objectivity that must grow into love, and as a matter of sheer logic we shall accept whatever they bring to us, in the way of joy or sorrow or responsibility, as coming from the hand of Christ; and because nothing comes from His hand that is not given for our ultimate happiness, we shall gradually learn that the things they do, the demands they make, all are part of God's plan for us. Once that is understood we can never again feel completely frustrated by anyone, or lose the serenity of our minds by nursing a grievance. Neither shall we ever again miss a joy that should have been ours through another person, because we dared not give ourselves to it, bravely. Parting too will lose its terrible power to afflict us, even the parting of death, for there will be no one whom we shall not find again in Him for eternity.

— *The Risen Christ, 32–33*

XXVIII

Put on Christ's Personality

It is a great part of our Christ-life to increase joy in the world, just as it is. First of all in our own lives, for joy must be a reality, something as deep and still and pure as water in a hidden well, under the ground. The forced smile of the amateur Christian is a blasphemy.

We cannot increase joy unless we "put on" Christ's personality, and our own joy actually is His.

. . . First of all its increase must begin in ourselves; we must grow in wisdom as Christ did, by deepening our understanding of the sacramental life, through the very substance of every day. Until there is nothing we see or touch that is not charged with wonder for us, though it is something as familiar as the bread on the table. And there is nothing that we do, though it be no more than filling a glass with water for a child, which does not sweep the loveliness of God's sacramental plan through our thoughts, like a great wave of grace washing them clean from sin and the sorrow that is inseparable from it.

Then we can increase joy through compassion, even where there is incurable suffering, for if we even want to put on Christ's personality we shall radiate His light, and He is the light which shines in darkness, which darkness cannot overcome.

— *The Risen Christ*, 60–61

XXIX

Mary's Yes

Christ asked Mary of Nazareth for her human nature. For her littleness, her limitations, flesh and blood and bone, five senses, hands and feet, a human heart.

He, who was invulnerable, asked to be able to feel cold and heat, hunger and thirst, weariness and pain. He who had all things and had made all things, asked to be able to be poor and to labor with His hands and look with wonder at the wild flowers. He who was wholly sufficient to Himself asked Mary to give Him a heart that might be broken.

. . . Our Lady answered "yes" to Christ; she answered for us all; she was quite human. Had He asked her for anything else but her littleness she could not have given it, because she had nothing else.

She gave Him human nature, our human nature; the Incarnation means that Christ gave Himself to human nature to be its supernatural life.

— *The Comforting of Christ*, 23–24

XXX

Christhood

We as Christians live with Christ's life. He lives our life, we are offered the glory of living His. But on earth it is impossible to respond to this offer, which involves loving with His love, without accepting what He accepted as man, that is, not only a fragment of the world's guilt, but all of it, all the suffering caused by sin, the world-sorrow. The suffering of the whole world is the concern of each one of us.

It is from the responsibility of guilt that modern man turns away, from the constant effort of self-conquest, from the acceptance of the world's suffering as his own business which he cannot shelve, and most of all from the mysterious destiny of his Christhood, with its imperious challenge to surrender himself body and soul to Christ's uncompromising, illimitable love.

———— ॐ ————

At first sight one would be tempted to say that He [Christ] had fallen in love with our suffering. He made Himself subject to our limitations—to discomfort, poverty, hunger, thirst, and pain. He chose to experience fear, temptation, failure. He suffered loneliness, betrayal, injustice, the spurning of His love, mockery, brutality, separation, utter desolation of spirit, the sense of despair, and death.

But it was not with our suffering that Christ fell in love; it was with us. He identified Himself with our suffering because He identified Himself with us, and He came not only to lead His own historical life on earth, but to live the life of every man who would receive Him into his soul, and to be the way back to joy for every individual. He took our humanity in order to give us His . . . .

Christ is "the Way." He taught the way to wholeness, showed it in His historical life, and He *is* the Way in the life of every individual who does not refuse his destiny of Christhood.

— *Guilt*, 16–17, 74–75

XXXI

The Host-life

In His risen life on earth Christ often made Himself recognized only by the characteristic of His unmistakable love; by showing His wounds, by His infinite courtesy, by the breaking of bread. He would not allow the sensible beauty and dearness of His human personality, His familiar appearance, to hide the essential *Self* that he had come back to give.

Wholly consistent with this is Christ's return to us in the Host. We know that in It He is wholly present, Body, Blood, Soul, Divinity. But all this is hidden, even His human appearance is hidden. He insists, because this is the way of absolute love, in coming to us stripped of everything but Himself.

For this Self-giving Christ, in the Host, is poor, poorer than He was when, stripped of everything, He was naked on the Cross. He has given up even the appearance of His Body, the sound of His voice, His power of mobility. He has divested Himself of color and weight and taste. He has made Himself as close to nothing as He could be, while still being accessible to us.

. . . Living the Christ-life means that we are given the power of Christ's love. We are not only trustees of God's love for man, entrusted to give it out second-hand, but, miraculously, *our* love IS His love!

"I have bestowed My love upon you, just as My Father has bestowed His love upon Me. Live on then in My love . . . ."[1]

The Host-life is an intense concentration of this power of love.

The Host-life is not something new or different from the Christ-life that we know already. It is the very core of it, and it was given to us at the Last Supper when Christ gave Himself to us in the Blessed Sacrament.

The Host-life is the life which Christ Himself is living in the world now. It is His choice of how to live His life among us today. At first sight it is baffling that it should be so.

Have *you* never stood before the Tabernacle and asked yourself: "Why is He silent, while the world rocks with blasphemies and lies? Why is He passive while His followers are persecuted and innocent people are crushed?"

It is almost frightening to seek an answer to the question: "Why does God remain in our midst silent and passive, knowing and seeing everything, but saying and doing nothing, while cruelty, injustice, ignorance and misery go on and on and on?"

It is a frightening question until we remember what it is which alone *can* restore humanity to happiness; that it is one thing only that can do it, namely supernatural life, beginning secretly in each individual heart; just as Incarnate Love began secretly on earth in the heart of Mary. It is one thing only, the birth of the Infant Christ in us, Incarnate Love.

. . . In the light of the Host-life, shining upon the modern world, it becomes clearly visible that the power of love, of comforting, of healing and alleviating suffering is given to the most unlikely people; to those who seem to be the most restricted; that the most effective action belongs to those who seem helpless and unable to do anything at all, and that there is a tremendous force of contemplation, unrecognized, but redeeming, in the midst of the secular world.

— *The Passion of the Infant Christ*, 123–25, 129

XXXII

Philip Speaks

The Lord blessed the bread.
He put it into our hands
and it multiplied,
not in *His* hands but in *mine*!
Even now, remembering this,
my thoughts shut like a folding wing;
my mind is a blank sheet of light
in the mystery of the thing.
I gave, and my hands were full, again and again;
pity in Him fell on my dry dust:
it was summer rain,
and the husk of my heart expanded and filled again

and was large with grain.
For me, the miracle was this:
that a clear stream of the Lord's love—
not mine—
flowed out of my soul,
a shining wave over my fellow men.[1]

— *The Flowering Tree*, 61–62

XXXIII

The Monstrance

For the moment, the precious and only *now*, you alone are the bearer of the Blessed Sacrament into your own little world. You are the monstrance, the priest giving Communion, the Real Presence, to your husband, your children and your friends; and the reason why, or one reason why, Christ has given Himself to you, is because He wishes to be with them, and can be with them, as things are, only through you. This is an astonishing thought, as every thought about the Blessed Sacrament is, if you bring an ounce of courage and realism to it.

Do you know the life of Charles de Foucauld?—a great symbol of many souls today . . . . He had never, in spite of the strongest possible urge to go into the desert and found a mission there, made any converts there (or anywhere, I think!), but he knew and said that his life, which was apparently fruitless, was wholly worth while, for one thing alone—namely, to take the Blessed Sacrament into the desert. He knew that if Our Lord was there in the Blessed Sacrament, He (Our Lord) would do there whatever He had come to do; that *He* is irresistible; and Charles de Foucauld did not think the sacrifice of everything, including his own life, too much to give for this end. It is precisely the same with us. There is nothing too much to do, in order to bring Christ in the Blessed Sacrament, as the sacramental life of our souls, into our own world, or home . . . .

— Letter to Mrs. Boardman, June 6, 1947,
The Letters of Caryll Houselander: Her Spiritual Legacy, 164–65

XXXIV

God's Purpose

When Our Lady found her son in the Temple at Jerusalem, she asked Him why He had submitted her and Joseph to this search.

He answered, "Did you not know that I must be about my Father's business?"[1]

That answers us when we ask the same question, and it answers the question: Why does Christ hide His glory and manifest Himself in humility, poverty, and necessity?

It is because He must be about His Father's business. His Father's business, the purpose of His life in human creatures, is to love and be loved.

That is the reason of our being in God; that is the reason of Christ's abiding in us. That is His sole purpose in man, to love and be loved.

Therefore Christ wants to be accessible: He wants to be disarmed of His glory so that the inglorious can come to Him without fear, so that He may come to the lowliest and least and be taken to their hearts.

For the same reason, He made the Host of the simplest of materials, unleavened bread, so little and light, so easy of access.

God's purpose is love; how to win the human heart, how to give it life.

There could not be a more ingenious way than the one He has devised, His way of hiding Himself in us, revealing His presence in our necessities, so that we can only find him by obeying His commandment: "Little children, love one another!"[2]

— *The Reed of God*, 105–6

XXXV

Christ: Man in Love

The part that the pain and privations of His body played in our redemption we know and meditate often: the poverty, the toil, the fasting, the crucifixion.

We think less often of the *joy* that should be ours through Christ's body.

It was the *Word* that was made flesh. Not only did He take our sorrows to Himself, but He gave the delight, the happiness that *He is*, to our humanness.

No man ever enjoyed life as He did. He gathered up the color, sound, touch, meaning of everything about Him and united it all to the most exquisite sensitiveness, the most pure capacity for delight.

Most people know the sheer wonder that goes with falling in love, how not only does everything in heaven and earth become new, but the lover himself becomes new.

. . . Christ on earth was a Man in love.

His love gave life to all loves. He was Love itself. He infused life with all the grace of its outward and inward joyfulness, with all its poetry and song, with all gaiety and laughter and grace.

With His body He united Himself to the world.

We incline to think that the comparison of Christ's oneness with His Church to human marriage is an attempt to find a symbol for *Christ's* love, that the marriage is the greater reality. But it is the other way about: the marriage of man and woman is the dim showing of the reflected glory of Christ's union through the giving of Himself, in the flesh, to humanity.

— *The Reed of God*, 62–64

XXXVI

How Joyfully Forgiving God Is

The whole meaning of the Mystical Body, Christ on earth, is that we *are* all "good with others' goodness" and guilty with others' guilt, praying with others' prayers, and so on. A soldier was talking to me the other day about a long route march he had made between two prison camps; he said something which seemed to me to be the most wonderful unconscious description of the Mystical Body, from the other angle, the angle of the Passion: "After we had been marching a long time, I didn't *feel myself* aching any more, I felt the tiredness of the chap behind me aching in my bones."

I think that's happened to you in a very big way and that you, thinking yourself frustrated from a part in the world's suffering, have ceased feeling yourself aching in you, because all the world is crowned with thorns in your mind; but then you should surely allow the prayer and joy and goodness of others also to come in—for otherwise it is "No" to Christ in them and a kind of thwarting of their love.

I fear I am being very confused.

My own feeling is that I must always look at God; I would not dare to form an ideal for myself and try to reach it, or to get a good realization of my sinfulness and dwell on it. Contrition, for my weak nature, must mean looking up and seeing how forgiving, and how *joyfully* forgiving, God is: adoration only, so to speak, turning in His direction.

> — Letter to a Young Friend Who Married and Settled Abroad,
> October 22, 1945, *The Letters of Caryll Houselander:*
> *Her Spiritual Legacy*, 114–15

XXXVII

Our Gift

It is a disconcerting fact that while the Lord who comes to us in Holy Communion is exactly the same person who will come to us on the day of judgement, we long for His coming in the one case and dread it in the other. We feel that we know Him instinctively now, but then He will be a stranger, that Christ the lover and Christ the judge are two different people. Of course they are not, they are one and the same, and in God justice and love are one and the same thing.

. . . We of this generation will hardly be able to ask on the day of judgement: "Lord, when was it that we saw thee hungry, or thirsty, or a stranger, or sick, or in prison—?"[1]

If for some reason we cannot take an active part in the works of love the world cries out for, we *can* recognize Christ in every man in every nation. We can close our minds against prejudice, we can live in communion with the whole world. We can pray in Christ's power.

If we have nothing material to give, we have poverty, if not bodily strength, we have weakness, if we have nothing else, we have ourselves. When Christ gave Himself, in the manger, on the cross, He was poor, naked, weak. He had only Himself. And what we have we can share with the nearest at hand, can divide with those who are in need with us.

The risen Christ was known in the breaking of bread. May He know us on the morning of our resurrection, through the breaking of our bread with humanity today. Today each of us will pass sentence on his own heart.

— *The Mother of Christ, 53, 55–56*

XXXVIII

The Prayer

Be born in us,

Incarnate Love.

Take our flesh and blood,

and give us Your humanity;

take our eyes, and give us Your vision;

take our minds,

and give us Your pure thought;

take our feet and set them in Your path;

takes our hands

and fold them in Your prayer;
take our hearts
and give them Your will to love.

— *The Splendor of the Rosary with prayers by Caryll Houselander*, 80

Notes

Foreword

1. Many sources say she was born in October, but in *A Rocking-Horse Catholic*, she says it was on the feast of Saint Michael.

2. *A Rocking-Horse Catholic* (New York: Sheed & Ward, 1955), 74.

3. Sidney Reilly, who was a prototype for Ian Fleming's James Bond.

4. *The Comforting of Christ* (New York: Sheed & Ward, 1947), 5.

III
God in Us

1. Forbidden.

VI
Paradox of Love

1. Gertrude Houselander had taken in a disgraced priest.

2. See Mk 14:26–31.

XI
Other Christs

1. See Jn 15:5.

2. Antacid tablet, sodium bicarbonate.

3. Ps 23:1.

XIV
The Tomb

1. See Mk 16:3.

2. See Mt 5:13–14.

3. See Jn 14:23.

4. See Lk 24:11.

XV
The Reception

1. Words from introductory dialogue of the Preface Prayer at Mass: "Lift up your hearts." "We lift them up to the Lord."

XVI
Delight in the Lord

1. See Ps 37:4.

XVII
Christ-life in the Soul

1. See the *Catechism of the Catholic Church* nos. 1258–1260. Those who die or are martyred desiring baptism, but before receiving the sacrament, are considered baptized.

XIX

I Am My Brother

1. Cheap lodging with few amenities; flophouse.
2. See Gen 4:9.

XX

The Risen Christ

1. See Mk 16:9–11.
2. See Lk 24:13–32.
3. See Jn 21:15–19.

XXII

Reaching Sanctity

1. See Jn 14:9.
2. See Lk 9:28–36.

XXVI

Showing Christ

1. See 1 Cor 12:1–31.
2. See Jn 15:4–5.

XXXI

The Host-life

1. See Jn 15:9–10.

XXXII

Philip Speaks

1. See Jn 6:1–14.

XXXIV
God's Purpose

1. See Lk 2:49.
2. See Jn 13:33–34.

XXXVII
Our Gift

1. See Mt 25:31–46.

Bibliography

Houselander, Caryll. *A Rocking-Horse Catholic*. New York: Sheed & Ward, 1955.

———. *Guilt*. New York: Sheed & Ward, 1951.

———. *The Comforting of Christ*: *Being a Peace-Time Edition,* rev. and enl. ed. of *This War Is the Passion*. New York: Sheed & Ward, 1947.

———. *The Dry Wood*. New York: Sheed & Ward, 1947.

———. *The Flowering Tree*. New York: Sheed & Ward, 1945.

———. *The Mother of Christ*. London: Sheed & Ward, 1978. Distributed in the United States by Christian Classics.

———. *The Passion of the Infant Christ*. London: Sheed & Ward, 1949.

———. *The Reed of God*. Westminster, MD: Christian Classics, 1985.

———. *The Risen Christ*. New York: Sheed & Ward, 1958.

———. *This War Is the Passion*. New York: Sheed & Ward, 1941.

———. *The Way of the Cross*. New York: Sheed & Ward, 1955.

Mayeski, Marie Anne, ed. *A Rocking-Horse Catholic*: *A Caryll Houselander Reader*. Kansas City, MO: Sheed & Ward, 1991.

———. *Women: Models of Liberation*. Kansas City, MO: Sheed & Ward, 1988.

Ward, Maisie. *Caryll Houselander: That Divine Eccentric*. New York: Sheed & Ward, 1962.

———. *The Splendor of the Rosary with Prayers by Caryll Houselander*. New York: Sheed & Ward, 1945.

———, ed. *The Letters of Caryll Houselander: Her Spiritual Legacy*. New York: Sheed & Ward, 1965.

Wright, Wendy M., ed. *Caryll Houselander: Essential Writings*. Maryknoll, NY: Orbis Books, 2005.

BOOKS & MEDIA

A mission of the Daughters of St. Paul

As apostles of Jesus Christ, evangelizing today's world:

We are CALLED to holiness
by God's living Word and Eucharist.

We COMMUNICATE the Gospel message
through our lives and through all
available forms of media.

We SERVE the Church
by responding to the hopes and needs
of all people with the Word of God,
in the spirit of St. Paul.

For more information visit our Web site:
www.pauline.org.

Pauline
BOOKS & MEDIA

The Daughters of St. Paul operate book and media centers at the following addresses. Visit, call, or write the one nearest you today, or find us at www.pauline.org.

CALIFORNIA

3908 Sepulveda Blvd, Culver City, CA 90230	310-397-8676
935 Brewster Avenue, Redwood City, CA 94063	650-369-4230
5945 Balboa Avenue, San Diego, CA 92111	858-565-9181

FLORIDA

145 S.W. 107th Avenue, Miami, FL 33174	305-559-6715

HAWAII

1143 Bishop Street, Honolulu, HI 96813	808-521-2731
Neighbor Islands call:	866-521-2731

ILLINOIS

172 North Michigan Avenue, Chicago, IL 60601	312-346-4228

LOUISIANA

4403 Veterans Memorial Blvd, Metairie, LA 70006	504-887-7631

MASSACHUSETTS

885 Providence Hwy, Dedham, MA 02026	781-326-5385

MISSOURI

9804 Watson Road, St. Louis, MO 63126	314-965-3512

NEW YORK

64 W. 38th Street, New York, NY 10018	212-754-1110

PENNSYLVANIA

Philadelphia—relocating	215-676-9494

SOUTH CAROLINA

243 King Street, Charleston, SC 29401	843-577-0175

VIRGINIA

1025 King Street, Alexandria, VA 22314	703-549-3806

CANADA

3022 Dufferin Street, Toronto, ON M6B 3T5	416-781-9131

¡También somos su fuente para libros,
videos y música en español!